SYMPATHY COLLECT

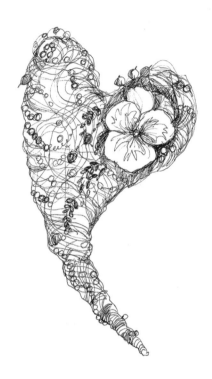

For Hannah *she knows why!!!*

First published in 2006 by Thrive Floristry, Coney Weston, Bury St Edmunds, Suffolk. IP31 1HG

Tel: 01359 221952
Fax: 01359 221952
Email: info@thrivefloristry.com
Website: www.thrivefloristry.com

Floristry: Claire Cowling ICSF MSF & Liz Cowling NDSF FSF
Photography: Peter Griffin, GGS Creative Graphics, Norwich, Norfolk. Tel: 01603 622500
Print: Reflex Litho, St Helen's Way Thetford, Norfolk. Tel: 01842 754600
Design Layout: Ben Cowling & Liz Cowling.

A catalogue record of this book is available from the British Library
ISBN No: 0954196090

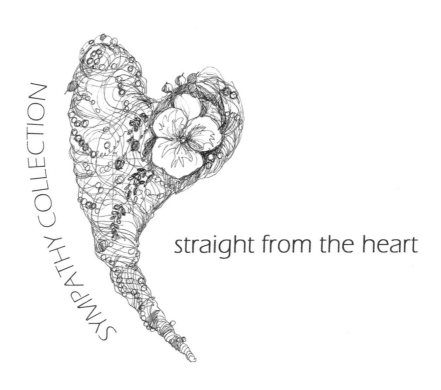

SYMPATHY COLLECTION

straight from the heart

Liz Cowling NDSF FSF
Claire Cowling ICSF MSF

To see a world in a grain of sand
And a heaven in a wild flower,
Hold infinity in the palm of your hand
And eternity in an hour.

William Blake

CONTENTS

INTRODUCTION

For centuries flowers have been given as tokens of esteem, condolence, and remembrance. Remember the stories from our childhood of the wreaths of flowers bestowed at the last resting place of heroes, paintings in caves showing regal lilies and lotus flowers? Or the garlands of flowers woven together in laurels and entwined in gold strips that were found perfectly preserved in the Pharaoh's tombs of ancient Egypt.

Flowers themselves express the feelings that so often words fail to convey, they speak a beautiful language without the complication of words, nor limitations of language. They are the perfect way in which to say a final farewell, and soothe a grieving heart, regardless of age, race or religion. They are windows into our soul; they convey the messages of friendship, love and hope, as well as increasing our appreciation and awareness of nature.

Today's funeral tributes are created using the time honoured symbols of the wreath, cross and heart, and brought right up to date with the subtle development of existing design techniques. The sterile and contrived shapes so popular of late make way for more gentle, emotive and meaningful designs and structured linear tributes which complement the form of the materials. The pristine bases of perfectly massed double white chrysanthemums are passe. The miles and miles of immaculately pleated polypropylene ribbon in synthetic colours are out of vogue. Stiff heavy sprays of perfectly straight stems are old hat.

Gentler, more sentimental funeral designs are always consoling. They celebrate the beauty of nature and natural materials and the continual cycle of life and the memory of them is enduring and lasts for much longer than the flowers themselves. Create tributes which are 'of the moment,' meaningful and emotive, which also reflects both the personality of the giver and the recipient, without resorting to the weird and wonderful, or compromising the flowers in any way.

Explore the beauty and possibilities of the symbolic shapes of the wreath, cross and heart using everyday materials.

Imagine. Try to visualize what would be most appropriate or fitting for a wide variety of people, in different age groups. Make their send-off's diverse – think of the type of coffin, ceremony and transportation as well as the age and preferences of the person. Far from being a morbid exercise it enables the florist to actually explore all kinds of possibilities without compromising their customers. It allows you to make the best of what nature has to offer – seasonally, by colour, trend and budget - yet has no physical cost. It is a highly valuable skill for the novice to master, as without 'understanding' it is virtually impossible to be able to interpret a customer's requirements and advise them effectively. The computations and possibilities are endless. The more you think about it the more ideas and possibilities present themselves, and the better prepared you are to offer professional and well informed, appropriate advice. Try it. Sketch down ideas and make notes of flower and colour combinations that would work well together. Other ways to see examples of how different people interpret a similar brief is to look at competition entries at the professional shows.

Ascertain likes and dislikes. Develop ideas.

Remember and practice the (floral) K.I.S.S. philosophy - 'Keep It Simply Stylish!' rather than overcomplicating design concepts or using too many techniques in a tribute. The flowers should be the stars... the message 'our thoughts are with you.'

Fashions may well come and go, but it is for certain that the giving of flowers will continue to be a perennial and necessary part of our lives. Enjoy discovering their extraordinary powers...

CONSIDERATIONS

Flowers can play an important role in celebrating a life. Final farewell tokens can be expressive and wholly individual whilst still being fit for purpose and within a given budget. Consultations may be difficult – especially with the newly bereaved – but are vitally important to ascertain all the relevant details and information as to what would be appropriate and in keeping with the style of service. No longer is a straightforward church service the main option – the style of coffin, the mode of transport, the readings and the music all are personal and so it is fitting that the floral tributes should also reflect the personality of the giver and the deceased rather than being just another cloned offering. It also makes it much more interesting for the floral designer to express individuality, whilst still retaining the natural beauty of the materials and the required return necessary for the success of the business.

There are many considerations to be made at the consultation. It is important to offer quiet, unhurried advice. Establish the formal details – the day, date, time and place of the funeral. The full name of the deceased, the name, address and delivery details of the undertaker, together with the required delivery time (this may be ascertained directly from the undertaker and may be dependent on several other factors - so never assume). The name, address and contact details of the customer.

Aside from the formal requirements essential to ensuring a straightforward business transaction there are several other considerations which need to be carefully thought about in order to quantify what is required, and hopefully create an ongoing relationship between the customer and the business. Ask about the type of funeral service – whether there are religious considerations to be made. It is probable that customers will volunteer information about the deceased, which is invaluable for enabling appropriate suggestions to be made. People die at all ages, from every imaginable scenario. So there is no fixed and straightforward right or wrong as to what is suitable. Flowers which are wholly appropriate for an elderly person would not necessarily be appropriate for an infant – yet how often do we see large, solid wreaths at babies' funerals – when a small dainty tribute would be far more appropriate? The first consideration from a professional point of view is to continually develop the ability to understand what would work well and be most appropriate and fitting, because it is only then that it becomes possible to move on from the contrived and formal tributes which have been around over the last twenty years or so.

Ascertain the client's particular likes and dislikes. Develop ideas.

Colour preferences are vitally important. Utilize all the lessons to be learnt from general studies of colour, as well as keeping a keen eye on current popular colour combinations, colours throughout the changing seasons and the influences of up and coming trends. Establish the kind of colour combination which pleases the customer as well as the style of tribute. For example - delicate, clashing, contrasting, subtle, all white, retro, feminine, masculine..... the possibilities are endless. Careful and effective use of colour is crucial not only for its visual impact but also its ability to add 'perceived value' to a design.

Consider the types of flowers and foliage which may be most suitable for the order – country, fragrant, exotic, classic, structural, long lasting, ethereal, bold..... again the choices and possibilities are endless – only restricted by our imagination in fact. The options can be enhanced by the effective combination and use of texture and form – ie consider using not only roses as a cut flower for example, but the use of petals in a variety of ways, thorns as natural fixings, buds of varying size and stage of development, seed pods and seed heads (some have gorgeous colours and textures) to add to the overall effect.

Consider the overall shapes which may be most appropriate for the

tribute - meaningful, religious, traditional, trendy.... Size matters – the overall dimensions of the tribute(s). In all cases the most important tribute is from the immediate family, so this should always be the 'focal.' Consider cost – it is not always the most expensive and time consuming tribute which is the most appropriate. Ascertain not only the volume of materials to be used, but also the make up costs, delivery and VAT. There is also the magical 'perceived value' which is vitally important to a successful business and which is achieved by mastering good design skills and effective, appropriate and efficient use of materials, colour and texture. Never underestimate the value of it. Keep a wide open, enquiring mind and an ever vigilant eye on what's available – interesting stems, leaves, straw, berries, bark, oh yes, and the flowers! Less is often more... use it effectively.

It may be that there are to be several tributes to be placed on the coffin, so if possible give ample consideration to the sizes and shapes so that they can be accommodated with ease. Consider the size of the coffin and suggest ideas which will complement it rather than over-whelm it – especially important for young children and infants. In these instances also think carefully of the sizes of flowers to be used – small headed materials would be far more suitable than large ones. For babies things like gypsophila, spray roses, Marguerites and lily of the valley would be far more suited than flowers like gladioli, large headed roses and chrysanthemums for example. The resurgence in choosing shapes and materials which have long held meanings is comforting in a world bereft of stability and which is continually changing. People remember the milestones in life. Not only do they remember the weddings, but they remember funerals. Flowers have always played an important role in these celebrations of life, in these changing times their significance is even greater. It may be wholly appropriate that the flowers are arranged for example as simple hand tied bunches or in baskets as opposed to the more formal shapes, or that dozens of tiny posies are strewn over the coffin, each bearing their own personal message.

The wreath is a tribute which has enormous design possibilities as well as being one of the most meaningful and beautiful shapes on which to work. The circular shape signifies never ending love which is totally appropriate. The design may be traditional, modern, casual, feminine, masculine, rustic, exotic or countless other styles as required. It may be made on a pre-formed foam base or constructed from natural materials and include lots of moss, twigs, branches and foliage as well as flowers. It's size can be small, modest or simply huge, and it's size is not necessarily dependant on cost. Appropriate for all types of funeral, all ages and all budgets.

The heart is a tribute which is best suited to close family members and wonderfully versatile for conveying heartfelt messages of love and affection. The tribute may be designed to be unashamedly romantic, casual, feminine, masculine or whatever is appropriate. Meaningful flower varieties may be included or suggested, however, often this approach can encourage the exclusion of some materials which when viewed purely for their intrinsic beauty would have been perfect accompaniments to other materials. Personally I feel that the meaning of flowers should be used with a fair degree of artistic licence. Colour is a brilliant way in which to emphasize romance, or passion, or feeling. Again the size may be small, modest or large, and not necessarily dependant on a large budget. Appropriate for all ages and all types of funeral.

The cross is a tribute which is highly significant and throughout history has had religious connotations. It is a perfect design where a religious significance is required and equally fitting as a family piece or an individual tribute. The style may be traditional, casual, rustic or formal, as appropriate. It is a perfect tribute in which to explore the use of berries, stems, moss and leaves as well as the more usual flower material.

It's a great shape for weaving techniques and simple designs. Appropriate for all ages, but most especially at religious ceremonies.

A coffin spray may be in lots of guises. Personally I prefer loose, casual styling in preference to stiff, contrived styles; however that is a purely personal choice – rather like making the choice between having a beautifully manicured lawn or one with a few daisies! Or a formal dinner in preference to a picnic! All have their place! The styling can be tailored to the client – casual, minimalist, exotic, rustic – whatever - and the stiffness of contrived design restricted, which gives a more natural feel. In nature nothing is exactly perfect; everything has its own little quirks and character. Celebrate and use the fact to advantage.

There are countless other ideas for coffin covers – blankets of flowers which drape across the width, tailored designs which accentuate the shape of the lid. Foliage garlands fastened around the sides – these are particularly good on wicker or bamboo coffins. Designs of varying sizes from family members connected with cords, vines or ribbon. Always consider the ease of transportation and practicality in these instances, as well as the tributes being entirely fit for purpose.

Small sprays and tokens are most suited as tokens of esteem from friends, relatives and acquaintances, and can be highly individual tributes even though often as a modestly priced one. The days of the basic single ended or double ended spray should be firmly numbered! There are thousands of ways in which to create sprays which are as individual as the people whom they are for. Not only does it make the wider public far more aware and appreciative of the significance and beauty of the flowers but it also makes the florist's job far more interesting and enjoyable.

Basket and hand tied designs are especially suited as either tokens of condolence or tributes. They are suitable for all age groups - young and old. Consider size, the cost and also the appropriateness, colours and styling of the materials being suggested for suitability.

Ensure that cards are neatly written and that all spellings are as the customer requires. In all instances place finished cards in cellophane envelopes to protect them. Fix them securely into the tribute along with the details of the deceased, making sure that they become an integral part of the design rather than sticking out like a flag.

It is also prudent to explain to the customer if a particular type of design or flower is not very long lasting. For example explain that rose petal tributes will last for a day or so only, whereas a foliage based design may last up to a month depending on weather conditions.

A well conducted consultation not only ensures that the customer's wishes are ascertained with regards to the floral tributes required at that time, but also lays good foundations for future business, which hopefully may be for happier occasions.

SYMPATHY COLLECTION

The time honoured symbol of the wreath conveys feelings of never ending love and affection, the circular form is emphasized by the addition of decorative wire bands. Flowers jostle playfully – the white signifies purity, the green, hope. It's a design of contrasts with strong bold shapes intermingled with fluffy delicate trimmings, which adds to the feeling of peace and tranquillity. Roses, chrysanthemums, gerbera, Lysimachia, Tanacetum and Physalis are all stunning for this tactile design. Other suggested materials may include dahlias, Phlox, Ranunculus, carnations, Trachelium, Bouvardia or lisianthus.

Tiny, immaculately formed hearts are simply gorgeous tributes, and just perfect either to or from children of whatever age. They can be decorated with loads of alternatives or left understated and ethereal. Golden wires may be added to highlight the form and add a little strength to the light and airy effect.

Contemporary designs using zillions of gypsophila flowers make cloud like pillows on which to arrange some carefully chosen blooms. Pristine trumpet shaped longiflorum lilies have to be one of the most popular flowers around, and together with a few softly coloured roses make a perfect combination for a modern tribute. The addition of bleached sticks and grasses adds to the 'of the moment' feeling and offers a welcome contrast in both texture and form.

Unashamedly romantic; a heart shaped design of roses, rose petals and seedpods. Dozens of softly coloured roses cluster tightly together; old fashioned subtly perfumed English garden roses from David Austin® the new 'Green' rose and mixed standard and spray roses whilst round the edges a tactile, romantic bed of rose petals softens the design. The piece is finished with long strings of rolled petals cascading over the bed of petals. A tribute surely 'straight from the heart?'

Other perfect combinations to consider may be reds - scarlet, through to crimson, ruby and near black, cerise through to deep red, creams through to golden yellow. In fact the possibilities are limitless!

Small basket arrangements convey heartfelt sentiments, when words fail.

Smart, luxurious and symbolic. This long lasting pair of tributes are made for each other, and portray never ending love and affection. The small heart combines textures and form with the emphasis firmly on foliage resulting in a soothing, quiet design, made extra special with the addition of three Phalaenopsis orchid blooms.

The wreath combines the symbolism of eternity and never ending love with an abundance of flowers and foliage cajoling together and decorated with a few choice Phalaenopsis blooms. The bear grass and decorative golden wires lead the eye round and adds the final finishing touch.

Classic designs with a modern twist add personality and individuality, and show that lots of thought has been put into the choice of the flowers and tribute.

The combination of white and green is reassuringly calming and comforting. The seemingly endless bands signifying the circle of life says 'I'll never forget you.'

Lots of flowers are wholly suitable and appropriate – choose your favourites. Roses, lisianthus, Ranunculus, carnations, marguerites, chrysanthemums, Phlox. Filler flowers could include Gypsophila, wax flower or Limonium.

A posy pad design brought up to date by punctuating the creamy white sea of carnations in the central section with individual Ornithogalum florets. The design is decorated with a band of choice and favourite flowers – roses, orchids and grasses. Various textures combine; playfully cajole together and contrast perfectly with the regular form of the centre section.

White and green is sophisticated and classic but other colour schemes would be just as nice. Try rich reds, sunny yellow, candy floss pink, vibrant cerise..... punctuate with berries or other small flowers...

Couture style designs – special but not overly extravagant and indulgent! These designs convey what words cannot. The soft colours harmonize, the careful placement illustrates perfectly sincere affection and regard.

Three roses enclosed and protected safely in a twiggy frame is just right as a small token of remembrance and condolence, or as a personal last farewell at the graveside. It is simple yet highly personal, and offers countless combinations for variation – both in colour and choice of materials to surround and protect the precious blooms.

In the bar shaped design the bleached sticks add strength to the delicate, frothy base structure of Gypsophila. Roses, carnations and grasses are placed carefully and lovingly atop. Rows of matricaria and flourishes of bear grass add the final finishing touches.

Similarly, the wreath is finished with a delicate spray which complements the frothy yet robust base of Gypsophila. Pastels are the ideal choice for these designs, but strong colours would be just as effective.

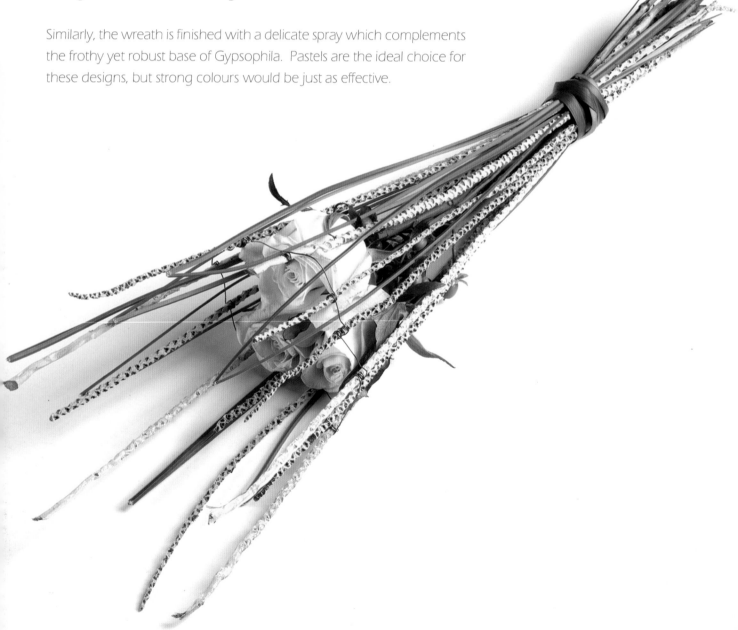

The timeless beauty of David Austin's® gorgeous old English roses teamed up with evocative country garden foliages and a sheer, wispy ribbon creates an emotive, unforgettable tribute reminiscent of days gone by. The loose, casual styling using flowing, trailing foliage creates a fitting paradise for the delicately perfumed roses.

It could be that you choose to have one rose to celebrate each year of your loved one's life, to make it even more personal and special. Alternatively, you may prefer an unlimited abundance to create your tribute. Either way it can only be truly special.

Ideal accompaniments might be rosemary, honeysuckle, lavender, dill, ivy, Alchemilla mollis, Phlox, Ammi majus, ferns, perhaps a Paeony or two...

A sea of classic creamy carnations make a soft cushion on which to place a floral ribbon made of Physalis, Amaranthus caudatus, rolled rose petals, tiny green chrysanthemums and bear grass in a zingy, fresh colour scheme. Perfect for using across a pillow as well.

Lots of small flowers and berries make a lush background on which to indulge a passion for choice roses in this highly individual posy pad design.

Country garden flowers in abundance make a tribute oozing with love and affection. The open heart is a traditionally styled design filled to bursting with gorgeous roses, and all kinds of summery flowers in a soft, dreamy colour combination. This design would also look luxurious in a selection of ruby red flowers, or all white.

Dozens of white asters give a retro feel to this substantial wreath which is relieved by some different textures - Physalis alkekengi, Antirrhinum and tiny white chrysanthemums.

Masculine, yet with *gentle tenderness* – these tributes use the distinctive forms of Anthurium with long curls of Eucalyptus bark as the basis for the designs. Wood stands for strength of character, bark for the constant rejuvenation of life, so both are wholly appropriate materials for inclusion. 'Miss Brown' Cordyline leaves add depth, form and structure to the calming colour combination. A few carefully selected roses, complementary flowers and berries complete the tributes, which can either be a bar shape or the more traditional and symbolic cross. The contrasting textures combine to create expressive, rustic tributes with a touch of the exotic. Vibrant red Anthuriums would create an exciting alternative colour combination.

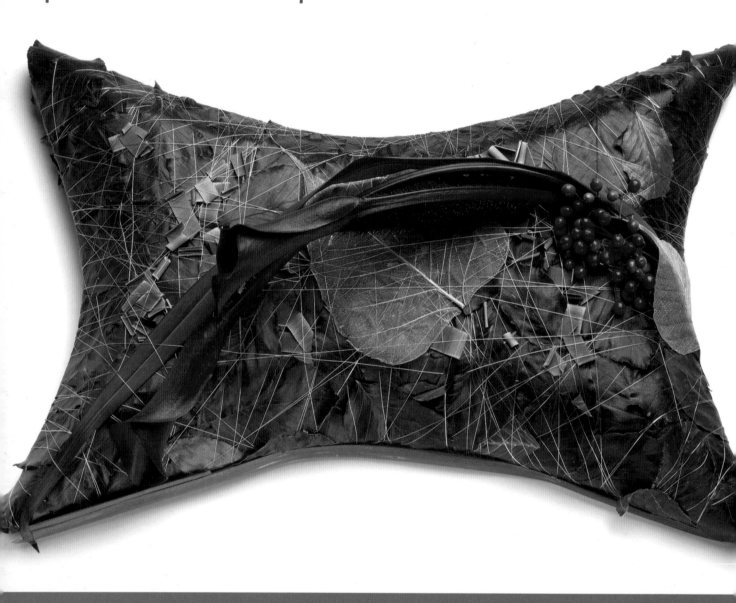

Copper beech leaves are bound randomly onto the pillow and chaplet as a base for tributes with lots of style and panache. Small pieces of Phormium tenax are bound on top of the beech leaves to offer a variation in shape and texture. Simplicity is the key to the design of the pillow, with a limited spray of Zantedeschia, Phormuim tenax, a cluster of Viburnum berries and a single stem of ornamental Millet "Purple Majesty" to give depth and texture. A pair of skeletonized leaves add yet another dimension and link with the gold binding wire.

The chaplet has a flourish of exquisite materials to embellish the simply covered base - a pair of richly coloured Zantedeschia together with trails of Amaranthus caudatus, Allium sphaerocephalon and pepper berries. Tightly bound golden straw crescents and bound lengths of Limonium emulate the shape of the spray and overall form and is completed with a single choice Phalaenopsis creating the focal point.

A simple basket design of dozens of dramatic Dendrobium orchids and steel grass provides a modest but striking tribute. Long lasting and exotic in nature, Dendrobium orchids are the ideal choice all year round and where vibrant colour schemes are favoured. Other flowers which could work equally as well with this type of styling would be small Phalaenopsis orchids, Craspedia or masses of rose petals.

Small green chrysanthemums are just perfect for retro style tributes; are long lasting, and as ever – green symbolizes hope. These designs are finished with strategically placed Dendrobium and Allium spaerocephalon flowers to add dramatic contrast, or a single choice Phalaenopsis orchid.

The large spray is an eclectic celebration of life, using a vibrant colour palette and several exotic blooms. Eremeurus, Dendrobium orchids, roses, Craspedia and Hypericum are complemented by sharp green Anthurium. Foliage includes Phormium tenax, Leucadendron, Panicum 'Fountain' and Aspidistra.

45

These structured designs focus on form, colour and texture. The dramatic form of Strelitzia, simple Zantedeschia and various Allium are rich and exotic set against the shiny textures of rolled Anthurium leaves, Aspidistra and ruscus.

The posy pad incorporates a gorgeous Protea and species Allium in stark contrast to each other and set snuggled down amongst the quieter areas of moss and berries.

Woven Ophiopogon leaves contrast with glossy Aspidistra leaves bound randomly with wire to create a distinctive alternative to the traditional open heart. This design is small and ideal where the mood is understated and a tailored design favoured. A single Phalaenopsis flower and delicate roses add a finishing flourish.

A simple tribute made entirely of Hebe - foliage massed and flowers is both gentle and calming. Many other materials could be used as an alternative including foliage and berries.

David Austin® roses are the stars in these tributes using quintessentially country garden flowers. The hand tied posy features several varieties of David Austin® English roses, together with a selection of standard roses, Lysimachia, Panicum 'Fountain', matricaria and lavender in a rich evocative colour scheme. An added bonus of the David Austin® roses is their fragrance. Roses symbolize eternity and are timeless expressions of love.

A natural cushion base formed from Muehlenbeckia has an abundance of roses atop to accentuate the shape. Buds, semi mature and open roses jostle happily together and sprigs of lavender complete the English country garden feel.

51

Crosses have been used for centuries as symbolic tokens of remembrance, and this interpretation uses the form to enclose and protect the flowers within. Gossamer fine leaves edged with decorative braid are used to create the edging. An opulent collection of flower material is massed and enclosed within using candy floss colours highlighted by rich carmine coloured roses. Flowers included are David Austin® roses, roses, hydrangea florets, lisianthus, Gypsophila and poppy seed heads.

Proteas make ideal small tributes when enclosed in a framework of protective decorative twigs. Strings of Protea petals, stamens and rose petals bound around the frame add the finishing touch.

A simple wreath of Eryngium takes on an extra special dimension with the addition of a floral ribbon decorated with vibrant Dendrobium orchids, rose petals and Protea petals and stamens. Many other wreaths would look dignified and consoling combining these techniques. Alternatives may include a base of carnations complemented by a ribbon of small orchids, rose petals and carnation calyxes. Or perhaps a base of soothing snugly bound foliage (bay or beech) with a ribbon of poppy seed heads, acorns, conkers and other found treasures.

Colours of summertime evoke happy memories of times spent together. Casual poses tied with sheer ribbon are suited as tokens of esteem and affection for the deceased or the bereaved. Mixed flowers in pastel colours – roses, Brodiaea, lavender, Gypsophila and grasses - snuggle closely together. Other suitable flowers may be lisianthus, Bouvardia, zinnias, Freesia, Astrantia, Godetia....

A full sized wreath overflowing with gentle pastel coloured flowers is a far more exuberant tribute than the posy yet retains all the casual easy styling, with just a hint more formality and symbolism. The wispy material balances the more solid forms of the Eryngium and roses; the colours are gentle and easy on the eye.

The combination in the cushion design is symbolic and meaningful – the cushion conveying peace, the massed rose petals expressions of love and intense feelings. Ivy represents eternity. The multicoloured rose petals are bound randomly onto the cushioned base with decorative wire. A couple of roses add a simple but poignant flourish. These tributes are not long lasting. Other possible variations could be creams/yellows/golds, reds, yellows/orange/rust, cream/oyster/peach.....

A handful of petals make a touching and sentimental gesture to be strewn on the coffin by the main mourners as the final good-byes take place.

Small posies of forget me nots and lily of the valley are meaningful and emotive tokens which are ideal for and from children.

Tiny casual hearts are just right as token gestures, or to and from children. Pinks have an old fashioned, gentle charm of their own – used en masse they need little adornment other than a few strands of grasses and tendrils of sweet smelling honeysuckle. Other flowers which may be suited to a small heart tribute may be spray carnations, hydrangea florets, small headed and spray roses, violets, forget me nots, marguerites, cheerfulness.

A traditional trug overflowing with David Austin® roses, roses, myrtle, lavender, ivy and fronds of fern is a thoughtful offering, which could be wholly appropriate as a sympathy gift or tribute. Rich reds and frothy pinks and mauves makes a loving, romantic combination. Other lovely choices may be all ruby reds, ruby reds and blues, all white, candy floss pink... loads of types of flowers are gorgeous for trug designs – think cottage garden – Phlox, forget me nots, roses, pinks, lisianthus, dahlia, peony, hydrangea, Ranunculus, Marguerites...

Dare to be different, whilst still retaining the symbolic gesture of the heart tribute. This tiny heart uses texture and form, grouping materials to make a tactile, emotive token, which may be small in size but is big in style. Lots of different materials are well suited – Gypsophila, matricaria, tiny roses, poppy heads, Crassula. Or how about, Hypericum berries, small headed chrysanthemum, pinks, Agapanthus florets, forget me nots?

The larger spray offers a notion of continuity and eternity with the use of bleached bands overlapping randomly through the quietly controlled design. A carefully chosen selection of choice flower material speaks volumes – colours are muted and gentle, textures and form varied. Flowers include roses, carnations, Gypsophila, Zantedeschia, matricaria, Alchemilla mollis, Amaranthus, Physostegia. Other combinations would work well, how about Ranunculus, Godetia, some varieties of chrysanthemum, lisianthus, anemones, Trachelium, Bouvardia, marguerites...?

Posies arranged in foam are great for lasting and modest tributes, and can be as casual or sophisticated as required. Mixed country garden flowers jostle for attention which says 'our thoughts are with you.' More sophisticated options may be to use an all white selection; Bouvardia, roses, small Zantedeschia or Ranunculus for example. For a sunny combination how about golden yellow roses, mini Gerbera, Freesia? Or a meadow collection of cornflowers, poppy seed heads and grasses...

Spheres of varying sizes make an avant garde, individual and dignified set of tributes where each member of the family could have their own choice of complementary or contrasting materials. The largest sphere is massed with creamy white carnations and decorated with a selection of favourite flowers and leaves – old English David Austin® roses, chrysanthemums, matricaria, Amaranthus caudatus, Allium spaerocephalon, Typha and other grasses. A finely covered gold wire encircles the sphere to signify eternity. Smaller spheres can be decorated similarly or each totally different reflecting the personality of both the giver and the deceased.

Candy pink Gypsophila has an altogether different look to the usual white and teamed up with lots of Limonium and a single David Austin® rose, stem of Amaranthus and grass it's an understated, no fuss tribute with bags of style. The same mix of flowers would also look great in heart shaped tributes, pillows, cushions and crosses.

Roses galore and lots of country garden flowers and foliage create a wild heaven in soft, dreamy colours. White, cream and a host of pink and soft blue materials create a loving and memorable tribute from the family. Gorgeous David Austin® roses are complemented by lots of standard roses, Ammi majus, Lysimachia, Eryngium and Molucella. Foliage and grasses used include Passiflora, wild oats and Viburnum.

Pure blue cornflowers and lots of mixed grasses make a casual and fitting tribute for a lover of the countryside and nature. Blues are restful and soothing, the flower combination reminiscent of happy, carefree days. Simple daisy shaped Marguerites make a stylish tribute in fresh white and green without being formal and staid. The folded steel grass makes a small design statement. This kind of casual wreath is great using a single type of flower, or how about a few meadow flower combinations? Maybe cornflowers in assorted colours – blue, pink and purple? All poppies - Papaver orientale together with lots of poppy seed pods and mixed grasses. Cornflowers in one or more colours, Marguerites and mixed grasses. Marguerites, forget me nots and mixed grasses. Marguerites, white Phlox and Alchemilla. Forget me nots, Nigella, marguerites and grasses... the choice is yours.

Tributes fashioned from a highly selective mixture of materials, colours and textures are ideal tributes for those requiring something a little different, or from companies and businesses. Scale can be tailored to suit both the budget and requirement. Long crescents of tightly bound golden straw form the basis of the design, which is then decorated with groups of materials. Zantedeschia and Phormium leaves follow the form giving a tangible sense of eternity and continuity. A pair of Phalaenopsis blooms enhance, finely covered decorative wires with tightly wound ends emulate the tendrils and vines - and add the finishing touches to a sophisticated design. Choose a rich colour scheme, bind corn ears with fine decorative wire to glint in the sunshine. Use rose seed heads for texture and form.

Classic is often best. Gorgeous white Longiflorum lilies teamed up with roses, ferns and Physalis make a timeless design suitable for all kinds of ceremony and ages. Bleached sticks and strands of steel grass placed randomly across bring the tribute right up to date, and makes it truly special. White flowers signify purity, green - hope.

A few stems of gorgeous Phalaenopsis orchids teamed up with heart-shaped Anthurium leaves creates an opulent, sophisticated and dignified tribute for someone special. It is classic yet with a gentle touch of the exotic, as well as being long lasting and casual in styling. Folded strands of steel grass makes an effective contrast to the larger, distinctive leaves, and beautiful flat faced flowers. Cymbidium orchids may be also suited to this style as an alternative. Other flowers which could be used in this way could be Anthurium, Zantedeschia...

Arums are a traditional flower used for remembrance and condolence throughout the centuries. Their classic and pure form need little adornment whether used in a modest sheaf style or a full scale spray.

Small garlands of tightly massed Gypsophila take away the stark simplicity of simple sheaf style tributes and add an individual, modern touch.

Rolled Anthurium leaves bound with fine gold decorative wire continue the funnel-shaped form of the Callas in the larger design. Teamed up with plain green foliage, Physalis and Molucella these tributes are sophisticated and symbols of hope and strength.

Pure white Zantedeschia grouped with a selection of creamy white roses and various grasses makes a peaceful and calming offering suitable for use as either a condolence or tribute. White signifies purity, green hope.

Using materials in an avant garde way, this heart shaped tribute is a modern, long lasting interpretation of a traditional favourite. The colour scheme of lime green and white on a base of copper beech leaves is striking and adds a touch of drama and originality. Lots of textures – leathery, raggedy, smooth, structured – all add to the clean, uncomplicated effect of the base. This design could be equally effective using a colour palette of cerise, terracotta or candy floss pink. Anthurium, Gloriosa, roses, chrysanthemum, Allium, orchids, Symphoricarpos and Ranunculus would all be great to use in this type of design.

Bright and cheery tributes bring a little bit of sunshine into the day. Beautiful tactile, golden roses complement the zingy fresh lime green Anthuriums, chrysanthemums and Physalis whilst the curious forms of Craspedia and Asclepia lighten the mood. Yellow is uplifting and for friendship, green is for hope. Willow and fine grasses emphasize the feeling of never ending love and affection...

It's near on impossible for happy faced sunflowers to not lift the spirits. Protected within a simple structure of bleached sticks, this simple tribute is an up to date version of the traditional sheaf.

Bark symbolized strength and when combined with cheery sunflowers, 'Cherry Brandy' roses and Eremurus it adds another dimension, and welcome contrast to the flower materials in this stylish spray.

The posy pad is long lasting as well as bright and cheerful. It's an ideal tribute, where a wreath, cross or more formal tribute is felt inappropriate. Other great things to use in this type of design to complement sunflowers may be berries, rosehips, bun moss, scrunched up autumn leaves, tightly bound crescents of hay, other kinds of bark, Sedum spectabile, Solidago, decorative maize...

If you like the unconventional whilst still keeping the theme natural and cheerful, then this wooden box filled with flowers may be just the thing for you. Clustered closely together lots of different textures and levels add interest.

A beautiful willow coffin is decorated in avant garde style using the centres of sunflowers, with groups of hydrangea, Sandersonia and roses in sunny golden and dusky pink colours. This tribute would remain fixed in place on the coffin.

Casual and easy on the eye, as well as soothing to troubled souls. Richly coloured roses have been teamed up with the lantern shaped Sandersonia, lots of grasses and a touch of Asclepias. Well suited as either a loving tribute for the deceased or as a message of condolence to the family.

Autumnal colours in a massed open heart design snuggle closely together. Nature's gems complement each other as light falls across the contrasting forms and textures. A few choice orchid blooms give the basis of the colour scheme - with roses, Viburnum berries, chrysanthemum, Gerbera, Craspedia, Physalis and grasses linking the whole together.

Structural groups of material in a strong colour combination make a highly individual and contemporary tribute, perfect as either a family piece or from a company. Crescents of straw form the basis of the design, complemented by strong bands of leathery Phormium leaves, glossy red berries, spherical Craspedia, roses, orchids and rustic, textural sunflower heads. Forms of tightly bound straw add a modern finishing touch. This design would also be gorgeous using a softer colour palette, with lots of contrasting textures.

Masculine, strong and yet traditional with a sense of the exotic. This design utilizes all the traditional features of the coffin spray together with a few new ideas. Leathery Anthurium, curiously beautiful Gloriosa and lantern shaped Sandersonia are the stars. Deeply coloured foliage brings richness and structure. Folded steel grass emphasizes the form.

Alternatively, a pillow based with copper beech leaves bound tightly with decorative wire makes an individual, poignant and meaningful tribute. The rich reds and varying forms and textures contrast strikingly with the randomly placed leaves. The overall effect is softened by light airy strings of cut steel grass and berries.

Crosses maintain a deserved popularity – when teamed simply with red roses and ivy they become ever more meaningful and poignant. Red roses are for love, ivy for constancy. Strings of rolled rose petals and Muehlenbeckia trails give a loose, casual feel.

Gorgeous red roses often require little embellishment or additional flower material to look their best and say what words cannot. A basket full of red roses cocooned in a trug shaped willow basket is suitable for both the bereaved or as a tribute. It may be that you choose a significant number of roses – perhaps one for each year of the deceased's life, or a particular variety of red roses, or maybe a mixture of several colours and forms of the red rose. The options are limitless. To finish folded steel grass add a contemporary touch.

Basket arrangements are highly appropriate; adding crescents of tightly bound hay gives a different dimension for the autumnal season along with various berries.

The possibilities are endless, spring flowers bursting through a bed of scrunched up leaves – Ranunculus, Cheerfulness, tulips, Hellebore, lilac... Sweetly fragrant summer flowers – roses, Nigella, Sweet William, pinks, peonies, Phlox, sweet peas, cornflowers, Marguerites, lots of grasses. For autumn – lots of berries, seed heads, autumnal leaves, Rudbeckia, chrysanthemums, Sedum, decorative maize... for winter – bare gnarled branches, cones, moss, stems of long lasting Cymbidium, Ilex berries, hyacinth.

Fragrant lilies team up with exotic heart-shaped Anthurium, gaily coloured Gerbera, carnations and lots of luscious foliage and berries in a traditional but styled coffin spray. Rolled Anthurium leaves bound with wire and a pair of exotic and distinctive Anthurium clarinervium leaves strategically positioned gives a contemporary touch.

David Austin's® beautifully cup shaped rose booms offer a luxurious and totally gorgeous accompaniment to standard commercial roses and spray roses. The hand fashioned heart of Muehlenbeckia provides a rustic base for the massed roses in shades of pink making them look a million dollars, and so English country garden.

A bed of dozens of David Austin® roses edged in a band of Gypsophila jostle playfully with fine stemmed Lysimachia and grasses making a fitting family tribute, which can be made in whatever colour scheme and shape is felt appropriate. The colours are gently contrasting, the roses are on different levels for interest and complemented by a selection of other flowers and a few wispy strands of sisal. This type of design would also be suited to using mixed types of roses, or roses and Paeonies for example. Or perhaps winter berries, mosses and cones, using an edging of ivy or bark.

Celebrate life with seasonal gems. Masses of Sweet William or Godetia in their distinctive summer colours are just perfect for a cheery, informal farewell.

An unashamedly romantic tribute which speaks volumes. Copper beech leaves topped with pieces of Phormium leaf are bound tightly with gold and cerise decorative wire to make a long lasting and distinctive base. The spray is a flourish of gorgeous roses, Gloriosa rothschildiana, Amaranthus caudatus and pepper berries. Strings of rolled rose petals are placed over the spray to finish.

Crosses are a traditional shape on which to express deep and meaningful feelings. Red is for love, bark the constant rejuvenation of life. Masses of rich berries form the basis of the tribute, which is edged with birch bark and strings of berries, and finished with a neat flourish of steel grass. It makes a striking and original tribute for someone special.

Alternatively, dress a berry base up with a selection of carefully chosen flowers. Rich red Amaranthus caudatus teams up with a few scarlet Gerbera, burgundy carnations and some choice Gloriosa. Shoestring ribbon visually softens the design.

Green is always calming, and treasures from the woods are appropriate for woodland burials. Mixed foliages - oak, beech, Thuja – together with other treasures such as conkers, poppy seed heads, cones and pieces of bark form the basis of this straw based design. Lengths of decorative wire and willow make never ending circles around the wreath. A ribbon of birch bark draped over the centre adds substance.

The materials on the coffin cover also give a peaceful, calming feeling. Softly coloured Anthurium, team up with sharp green chrysanthemums, Hypericum berries, grasses and Physalis. A birch bark ribbon unites the basket and the flowers. This design would remain fastened on to the basket.

Christmas is a time for remembrance, and long lasting tributes of mixed winter foliage, cones and cinnamon are ideal for the possible adverse weather conditions. Add in treasures such as rolled Eucalyptus bark and perhaps a single rose or two.

A bang up to date, contemporary version of the well loved, traditional holly wreath utilizes the leaves singly rather than in sprigs. Sturdy Leucadendron leaves add a bit of contrast to the base, giving it a more Christmassy feel. A single meaningful red rose and rolled rose petals add the message 'We will never forget you." Perhaps choose a yellow rose to remember a friend.

PREPARATION

Floral foams are great water retaining products, which assist the designer to arrange flowers and at the same time prolongs the life of the flower materials used. Smithers Oasis® products are at the forefront of this technology. To obtain maximum results and benefits from the foam, you will need to do the following:

Ensure the container that you soak the foam in is clean and large enough – depth and width wise - for your foam or frame to soak properly. After filling the container with enough water depending on the size/number being soaked (a standard size brick holds approximately two litres of water), add the correct dosage of cut flower preservative. Next float the OASIS® brick or frame on top and allow to take up the water by itself. Do not push the foam down under the water as this will create an air lock and you will have an area of unsoaked foam from which the flowers will not be able to hydrate. Saturation time of foam varies, depending on the density of the floral foam and the size of the piece, but as a general rule, a standard size brick of OASIS® floral foam saturates in less than one minute. Do not oversoak.

When you have soaked the foam (and if required fixed it into your container, depending on the style of your chosen design), you may need to chamfer a little from the edges of the top and sides. This gives you a better overall profile and surface area to work on. Some designs may need to be kept in the original form if they require a squarer profile rather than rounded.

Cut all materials to be used with a clean, slantwise cut using a sharp knife, and remove all lower foliage so that you have a clean stem to insert into the foam. Ensure that your material placements are inserted well in (at least 2.5cm), so that they stay in position, but more importantly so that they can reach a constant water supply. Should you need to reposition a stem, reinsert it into the foam in a fresh place to avoid an air pocket which would prevent the stem from hydrating.

Finally, where possible keep your foam topped up with a mix of fresh water and flower food. Spray with either a mist sprayer or a flower preservative. Always check the whole tribute before delivery.

MATERIALS & METHODS

18

Rose
Chrysanthemum 'Shamrock'
Limonium overig 'Emille'
Tanacetum parthenium 'Snowball'
Gerbera
Chrysanthemum santini 'Yoko Ono'
Lysimachia clethroides
Physalis alkekengi
Hypericum 'Green Condor'

Mixed foliage
Foam Frames® wreath frame
Taped stub wires
Fine decorative reel wire

Make a loose wreath with a variety of materials using lots of recession & transition. Add a very few strands of sisal to soften and increase the feeling of continuity by adding several long wires which have been tightly bound with sprigs of Limonium.

20

Gypsophila paniculata
Rose
Steel Grass
Foam based heart frame

Prepare base as usual, chamfering the edges before inserting flower material. Base the heart evenly with tiny sprigs of Gypsophila. Finish with a single flower of your choice and a couple of pieces of steel grass.

Gypsophila paniculata
Bleached willow sticks
Longiflorum lilies
Panicum 'Fountain'
Rose 'Sereno'
Setaria italica
Steel grass
Double spray tray
Pot tape

OASIS® ideal bricks
Wires

Prepare tray and foam. Cover the entire shape neatly with sprigs of Gypsophila, ensuring the base tray is not visible. Make a random criss cross pattern with the sticks and fasten neatly with stub wires. Insert the flower material making sure a mixture of buds and open flowers are used. Finish with a flourish of steel grass.

21

Gypsophila paniculata
Rosebuds
Poppy seed heads
Brachyglottis
Xerophyllum tenax
Stub wires
Decorative reel wire
Skeleton band

Prepare base and chamfer edges before inserting flower material. Base the heart using small sprigs of Gypsophila. Decorate using a few taped stub wires which have been bound with fine gold reel wire. Follow the shape of the heart with a few pieces of skeleton band, a few silvery Brachyglottis leaves, beargrass and flowers as desired.

23

Roses – various varieties as desired. Include several different types and forms. 'Green,' 'Talea,' 'Akito,' David Austin® roses and spray rose.
Foam Frames® heart frame
Decorative reel wire
OASIS® floral adhesive
Sisal

Prepare the base as normal, and chamfer edges. Cover the outside (approx 5cm's from outer edge)of the frame with teased sisal bound in place with decorative reel wire, then rose petals. Attach some single rose petals on top with cold glue, making sure that it is even all round. Leave stems of main roses approx 60-80mm long, fill in the centre section, varying heights and variety for interest. Use seedheads and tiny, immature buds as well. Make strings of rolled rose petals and drape around edges, fastening securely in place.

24

Rose 'Akito'
Hypericum
Phalaenopsis
Typha grass
Eucalyptus bark
Basket
OASIS® Ideal brick
Pot tape, stub wires & cold glue

Prepare as normal, and fasten foam securely into basket. Mass roses, keeping heads level. Add interest to the outside using a few pieces of Eucalyptus bark fastened with stub wire, a few of pieces of Hypericum and some Typha grass. Add a special touch by gluing an orchid to the handle.

24

Phalaenopsis orchids
Conifer 'berries'
Various foliage including Brachyglottis, Hedera, Hebe
Lavender
Pepper berries
Xerophyllum tenax
Small open heart frame
Fine decorative reel wire

OASIS® floral adhesive

Prepare the frame as usual. Chamfer the edges of the frame to give a good shape and area to work on and then bind single leaves securely on to one side with decorative reel wire, (use the reverse side as well as top side of leaves for variation). Complete the rest of the base in a textured style. Finish with choice orchid flowers and a few flourishes of bear grass. Accentuate the leaf section with conifer berries.

25

Gypsophila paniculata
Rose 'Bianca spray' and 'Sereno'
Poppy seedheads
Alchemilla mollis
Foliage & few strands of Xanthorrhoea australis
Foam Frames® wreath frame
Taped stub wires
Fine decorative reel wire

Phalaenopsis orchids

Prepare frame as usual, chamfering the edges prior to inserting flower material. Make the wreath using the techniques for a loose wreath. Bind long, taped stub wires with decorative reel wire; insert them around the wreath carefully to accentuate the shape and form of the wreath. Add strands of bear grass in similar fashion and complete the design with some orchids to add a special finishing touch.

26

Roses
Lathyrus odoratus
Lisianthus
Dianthus barbatus
Various foliage, grasses & vines
Few strands Xanthorrhoea australis
Foam Frames® posy pad
Bleached cane

Prepare the frame as usual, chamfer the edges prior to inserting flower material. Arrange the flowers and foliage as desired, ensuring that you recess some materials for interest. Secure lengths of flat cane in a circular fashion over and around the design. Emphasise with vines, grasses and bear grass fastened in a circular manner to finish and accentuate the movement within the design.

27

Rose 'Bianca' spray
Hydrangea
Alchemilla mollis
Gyposphila paniculata
Various foliage
Poppy seedheads
Foam Frames® wreath
Skeleton Band
Flat cane

Prepare the frame as usual, chamfer the edges, prior to inserting flower material. Make a loose wreath using a variety of flower and foliage types, and lots of textures and forms for interest. Bind over with strips of cane and skeleton band to emphasise the round form and movement within.

29

Carnation
Rose
Phalaenopsis
Ornithogalum arabicum florets
Philadelphus
Grasses
Various foliages
Xerophyllum tenax
Foam Frames® posy pad frame

Sisal
Flat cane
Natural cane

Prepare frame. Do not chamfer edges. Base the centre section of the with carnations. Around the outside add flowers and foliage. Emphasise the circular form by adding bear grass, varying types of cane and vines to finish. Accentuate the centre by gluing Ornithogalum florets in a regular pattern. A little sisal softens the outer decoration.

30

Roses
Steel grass
Typha grass
Decorative Sticks
Decorative reel wire
'Polybast

Make a frame using the sticks, binding them in place with standard gauge reel wire. Insert the roses inside, decorate with a few pieces of steel grass and tie off. Neaten the tying point with Typha grass, secured in place.

31

Gypsophila paniculata
Bleached willow sticks
Rose 'Talea'
Carnation
Tanacetum parthenium 'Snowball'
Setaria grass
Xerophyllum tenax
Double spray tray
Pot tape

Oasis® ideal bricks
Wires

Prepare base. Cover the entire shape neatly with sprigs of Gypsophila. Make a criss cross pattern with the sticks – having a mix of short thicker pieces and narrow longer lengths and fasten in place with wire. Insert the flower material in clear, block line placements. Finish with a flourish of bear grass, a few grasses, and 'button-like' detail of Tanacetum for fun and interest.

31

Gypsophila paniculata
Roses 'Talea'
Hydrangea
Physostegia virginiana 'White Discovery'
Bear grass
Foam Frames® wreath frame

Prepare the frame as usual and chamfer the edges. Base the frame thickly with sprigs of Gypsophila. Add a subtle spray to one side keeping the materials fairly short and integrated into the base work, as opposed to sitting on top of the base work. Finish with a single rose enhanced by a couple of bear grass loops and criss crossed bear grass over the spray section.

33

David Austin® roses – various varieties
Tanacetum parthenium 'Snowball'
Lavender
Lysimachia clethroides
Allium sphaerocephalon
Various foliage & grasses
OASIS® Masterboard
Organza ribbon

Prepare base and make a loose, casual spray in usual way. Make sure to include lots of feathery, trailing material for best effect. Add a final finishing touch of gossamer fine ribbon trails, with knots about 100mm from ends. Do not make bows, as this tends to make the overall effect rather old fashioned.

Dianthus
Amaranthus
Chrysanthemum santini 'Yoko Ono'
Physalis alkekengi
Antirrhinum
Chamelaucium
Foam Frames® cushion base
Decorative reel wire

Firstly prepare the frame and chamfer edges. Insert carnations into base neatly. You may find it easier to split the calyxes and pin into place with German pins, especially at the sides. Prepare strings of various materials on fine decorative reel wire and drape across the cushion for interest – Antirrhinum flower heads, Physalis lanterns, rolled rose petals and so on. Spray with flower preservative.

David Austin® roses
Rose
Hypericum
Limonium
Ammi majus
Asparagus umbellatus
Chamelaucium
OASIS® Posy pad frame

After soaking frame, chamfer the edges and insert the main spiral of roses. Then add the next placements of flowers in a similar manner and following the spiral. For the outer area, fill with random placements of smaller dainty flowers & foliages to soften the look of the overall piece.

David Austin® rose 'Juliet'
Rose 'Bianca'
Spray Rose 'Sereno'
Allium sphaerocephalon
Ammi majus
Lavender
Tanacetum parthenium
Poppy heads
Various foliages

Foam Frames® open heart frame

Prepare frame in the normal way and chamfer edges. Define the outline shape with foliage. Next add the main roses to the upper part of the design, in grouped placements at varying heights. Complete the form with smaller flowers in interesting groups and levels.

Aster
Chrysanthemum
Physalis alkekengi
Antirrhinum
Various foliages

After soaking the frame and chamfering the edges, add placements to foam in a casual way, recessing some and having a little more height with others – bringing visual interest, colour shape and size of materials.

Roses
Anthurium
Honeysuckle
Hypericum
Eucalyptus 'Baby Blue'
Eucalyptus bark
Various foliage including Cordyline 'Miss Brown'
Spray tray

OASIS® ideal brick
Pot tape

Secure a half brick of foam to the tray using pot tape. Develop the overall shape with bark curls and main foliages, creating varying levels and layers. Add shorter foliage, keeping within the profile and finish with careful placements of flowers – some bold and striking, other less dramatic.

Roses
Anthurium
Sandersonia
Hydrangea
Dianthus
Hypericum
Sedum 'Matrona'
Eucalyptus 'Baby Blue'
Eucalyptus bark

Various foliage including Cordyline 'Miss Brown'
Flat moss
Foam Frames® Cross
Stub wire

First define the overall shape and profile with the Eucalyptus bark. Next add flowers, foliages, berries and moss in a textured and grouped manner, giving lots of visual impact and interest and finish with grass to accentuate the cross shape.

Fagus sylvatica 'Atropunicea'
Zantedeschia
Phormium tenax
Viburnum opulus 'Compactum' berries
Ornamental grass 'Purple Majesty'
Foam Frames® pillow base
Skeleton leaves
Black pins
OASIS® floral adhesive

Fine decorative reel wire

Begin by chamfering the frame to the desired shape and profile. Next, lay Fagus leaves onto frame and secure by binding with fine reel wire. Add cut pieces of Phormium tenax for visual interest and fix. Place Callas and Phormium leaves into the foam and berries and millet for interest and depth. Finish edges with Phormium leaves and complete design with skeleton leaves.

41

Fagus sylvatica 'Atropunicea'
Zantedeschia
Allium sphaerocephalon
Amaranthus
Pepper berries
Limonium
Foam Frames® chaplet base
Straw
Fine reel wire

Black pins
German pins

Prepare base and chamfer the frame to desired profile. Cover with beech leaves and fix by binding with reel wire. Emphasize the overall form and spray with lengths of bound straw and Limonium. Complete design with clean and simple spray.

43

Dendrobium Orchid
Xanthorrhoea australis
Flat moss
Basket
OASIS® Ideal bricks
Bleached willow
Oasis® floral adhesive

Prepare and fix foam into your watertight basket as usual. Add a layer of flat moss to mask the foam. Add sticks at varying levels and lengths. Add steel grass – bending to give a good profile and movement. Add Dendrobium orchids – some as full stems, other glued onto steel grass.

44

Chrysanthemum santini 'Yoko Ono'
Dendrobium/Phalaenopsis Orchid
Allium sphaerocephalon
Liriope gigantean
Xanthorrhoea australis
Foam Frames® wreath ring
OASIS® floral adhesive
Stub wire

For both designs prepare the frame and chamfer the edges. Then randomly base the frame with santini using varying layers and head sizes for visual interest. You may need to support wire some stems! Finish with Dendrobium, Allium and lily grass or perhaps a choice Phalaenopsis Orchid (and a few strands of grass!).

45

Anthurium
Dendrobium
Rose 'Sphinx'
Craspedia
Eremurus
Leucadendron
Foliage includes Fatsia, Asparagus umbellatus, Aspidistra, Eucalyptus
OASIS® Masterboard

Prepare base as usual. Start with the larger structural leaves to build up the basic shape. Add main flowers, allowing space and depth within the design. Fill in with shorter flowers and foliages. Finish with softer grasses.

47

Zantedeschia
Strelitzia reginae
Allium sphaerocephalon
Hypericum
Various foliages to include Anthurium crystallinum & andreanum, Aspidistra & Liriope gigantean
Smithers Oasis® double spray tray
OASIS® Ideal bricks

Fine decorative reel wire
Pot tape

Secure foam to tray. Build up outline shape with strong leaves. Add flower materials in groups working through the design. Fill in with shorter materials. Finish with lily grass to soften.

47

Protea
Allium christophii
Rose
Zantedeschia
Carnation
Phormium tenax, Steel grass
Viburnum opulus 'compactum' berries
Ornamental grass 'Purple Majesty'
Anthurium andreanum & crystallinum

Hypericum 'Verocla, Bun moss
Foam Frames® posy pad frame
Decorative reel wire

Prepare frame, do not chamfer edges. First add areas of moss and leaves – both flat and rolled. Next add main flowers, giving plenty of recession and careful placements of flower groups. Insert Phormium leaves into foam and fix around the frame. Fill in and finish the design with some decorative features of threaded hypericum berries.

48

Ophiopogon nigrescens
Aspidistra
Phalaenopsis Orchid
Spray rose 'Sereno'
Crassula 'marnieriana'
Open heart frame
Black pins
OASIS® floral adhesive
Coloured reel wire

Begin this design by chamfering off the edges of the presoaked frame to give a good shape, then weave the bulk of your Ophiopogon area checking that it is wide enough to cover the side of your frame. Attach to the frame using black pins. Add Aspidistra leaves to the other side, fixing in place with reel wire. Finish with a small and stylish spray – a single accent Phalaenopsis bloom, spray rose and foliages – with a few strands of Ophiopogon to carry the design concept through.

49

Hebe speciosa
Hebe diosmifolia
Xanthorrhoea australis
Foam Frames® wreath

First you will need to sort out your Hebe! Starting with a stem, remove and put into piles 1. open flowers, 2. tight buds 3. just foliage. Take your soaked frame chamfer the edges and starting with one pile of materials ie 1. open flowers, insert into foam following the circle in a one directional movement. Next add the next section.. and so on. To echo the movement in the design, accentuate with curving lines of steel grass.

50

David Austin® Rose 'Miranda'
Rose 'Cool Water' & 'Sanaa'
Lavender
Matricaria
Lysimachia
Setaria grass
Panicum 'Fountain'

Strip lower foliage from materials to ensure a clean to the bouquet and binding point. Make your hand tie in the usual fashion ensuring the stems are neatly spiralled. Tie off and finish wit sheer ribbon.

51

David Austin® Rose 'Miranda'
Rose 'Cool Water' & 'Sanaa'
Spray Rose 'Sereno' & 'Diadeem'
Lavender
Muehlenbeckia base
foam Frames® cushion
Skeleton band
Skeleton Leaf
Reel wire

Sisal

Shape the vine into desired shape and add foam. Secure into place. Add mixed shapes, forms, size and colours of roses onto the cushion. Finish with skeletonized leaves, sisal fibres and lavender to soften.

52

David Austin® Roses
Rose 'Cool Water'
Lisianthus
Poppy heads
Gypsophila
Foam Frames® cross frame
Skeleton leaves
Ribbon & braid
OASIS® floral adhesive

Prepare foam frame in the usual way but do not chamfer edges. Fix skeletonized leaves to the frame with glue and add braid to neaten. Fill with textured placements of flower material. Finish with long, trails of fine shoestring ribbon.

52

Protea
Rose
Decorative sticks
Decorative reel wire

First construct the framework by fixing decorative sticks at two levels with reel wire (matting style), leaving more space at the top. When your circle is complete, add the Protea and fix in place with reel wire. Decorate just at the base of the Protea flower with chains of Protea stamens, petals and rolled rose petals. Spray with flower preservative to retain moisture.

53

Eryngium
Rose (petals)
Dendrobium
Protea
Poppy heads
Foam Frames® wreath frame
Wire mesh band
OASIS® floral adhesive

Prepare frame in the usual way and chamfer the edges. Make wreath with massed Eryngium. Either use a ready made wire mesh band or make one to suit using stub wires. Fix the band securely to the base frame. Decorate by gluing petals and flower heads to the mesh ribbon.

54

David Austin® Roses
Rose 'Cool Water'
Matricaria
Lisianthus
Gypsophila
Amaranthus
Brodiaea
Panicum & Setaria grass
Ribbon

Polybast

Strip lower foliage from materials to ensure a clean stemmed bouquet and binding point. Make your hand tied bouquet in the usual fashion ensuring the stems are neatly spiralled. Tie off and finish with a sheer ribbon.

55

Gypsophila
David Austin® Roses
Roses
Lisianthus
Eryngium
Broody
Various foliages & grasses
Foam Frames® wreath

Prepare the frame in the usual way and chamfer the edges. Start by loosely basing the frame with Gypsophila, then arrange materials in a casual manner. Add a few strands of steel grass for movement.

56

David Austin® Roses
Roses – various varieties
Hedera
Foam Frames® cushion base
Fine decorative reel wire
Sisal
OASIS® floral adhesive

Soak the frame and chamfer the base to give a good profile, add sisal fibres to the edge to disguise the frame then add layers of petals. Secure in place with fine reel wire and glue if required. Decorate with a couple of roses and a trail of ivy.

57

Various roses including David Austin® roses
Basket

Fill a basket with a selection of rose petals, small roses and seed heads. Make sure that the varieties chosen are not too soft and fragile. Spray with a flower preservative.

58

Myosotis
Convallaria majalis
Rosemary
Asparagus smilax
String
Ribbon

Firstly remove the lower foliage from the materials. Arrange in a hand tied posy and add smilax to outer edge for a dainty collar. Tie off and finish with a suitable ribbon.

58

Dianthus
Lonicera
Xanthorrhoea australis
Setaria grass
Small heart frame
Pepper berries
Sisal
OASIS® floral adhesive

Place pinks into foam using a variation of open flowers and stages of buds. Secure a small amount of sisal to outer edge to mask base, then decorate with Pepper berries, foliage trails and grasses. Finish by gluing Lunaria giving a different texture and transparent feel to the piece.

59

David Austin® Roses
Rose 'Black Baccara'
Spray Rose 'Diadeem'
Eryngium
Lavender
Various foliages to include Myrtle, Eucalyptus & Hebe.
Trug basket
OASIS® Ideal brick

Angel Hair
Pot tape

Prepare trug and fasten soaked foam into place. Build up the outline shape with foliage. Add flower materials. Finish with a twisted length of Angel hair.

60

Spray Rose
Matricaria
Crassula marnieriana
Gypsophila
Hedera
Poppy heads
Xerophyllum tenax
Small heart frame
Black pins

Prepare the base and chamfer edges. This design has textured groups of materials – so start by adding these – at varying levels for visual interest. When the bulk of your frame is covered, decorate the outside with smaller leaves (which can be pinned if desired). Materials such as Crassula can also be removed from their stem – and then pinned through the centre. Add a few strands of bear grass to finish.

61
Rose 'Talea'
Dianthus
Zantedeschia
Matricaria
Gypsophila
Physostegia virginiana 'White Discovery'
Poppy heads
Amaranthus, various foliages
Steel grass, Setaria grass

Double spray tray, OASIS® Ideal bricks
Pot tape, Flat cane

Prepare the base as usual. Begin by roughly masking the foam with foliage. Add flat cane – varying lengths and levels, overlapping and intertwining through the overall design. Add main flower placements with some recessed others more prominent. Finish by adding flowing materials – callas, Amaranthus, grasses – all overlapping through and over the design. Make sure all foam is covered.

62
David Austin® Rose 'Juliet'
Rose 'Akito'
Spray Rose 'Diadeem'
Allium sphaerocephalon
Marguerite
Amaranthus
Lavender
Hypericum
Various foliages

Foam Frames® posy pad frame
Decorative reel wire

Prepare the base as usual. Loosely cover the base with foliage. Add the main flower materials in an informal, but slightly grouped manner. Finish with a few strands of lily grass around the outer edge, giving movement and threaded berries & steel grass garland over the center for interest.

63
David Austin® rose 'Juliet'
Rose 'Talea,' spray rose 'Sereno'
Allium sphaerocephalon
Tanacetum parthenium, Dianthus,
Chrysanthemum santini 'Yoko Ono'
Sedum 'Matrona,' Amaranthus
Setaria grass, Lily grass
OASIS® Spheres
Decorative wires

Soak spheres. Cut a small section off the base so that they sit flat. Cover with a large leaf and secure in place. Mark out your area for the detailed section of the design. Start by placing carnations to the outer area. When complete, add an interesting mix of materials to the top; grouping placements. Finish by adding some decorative wires and lily grass. The smaller spheres are made in a similar fashion – basing with santini, and adding a line feature throughout the design of spray roses and gold covered wires. As an alternative wrap the sphere with leaves and decorate the top with roses and vines around to soften.

64
Gypsophila
David Austin® Rose 'Miranda'
Amaranthus
Limonium
Panicum fountain & Setaria grass
Steel grass
OASIS® wreath frame

Soak the frame and chamfer the edges. Base the frame thickly with pink gypsophila and Limonium, making sure that the foam is well covered. Add a single gorgeous 'Miranda' Rose, with soft foliage to enhance as an accent.

65
David Austin® roses
Roses – various
Spray Rose
Matricaria
Allium sphaerocephalon
Ammi majus
Sedum 'Matrona'
Amaranthus
Eryngium

Various foliages & grasses
Smithers OASIS® Masterboard

Soak base. Define the shape of the spray with foliage. Add flower material in casual line placements throughout the design, making sure some are recessed – giving interest and a good overall profile.

67
Marguerite
Brachyglottis greyii
Xanthorrhoea australis
Foam Frames® wreath

Prepare frame and chamfer sides. Begin inserting Marguerites and foliage into foam – a section at a time, to ensure even placement. When the circle is complete, add a few pieces of steel grass across the design, giving a clean, fresh look.

67
Centaurea cyanus
Setaria grass
Xanthorrhoea australis
Various foliages, vine & grasses
Foam Frames® wreath

After soaking & chamfering the frame, loosely mask base with foliage, grasses and vines. Next add the Steel grass bending the stems and inserting back into foam – giving depth and movement within the design. Finally, add the Cornflowers ensuring that they are placed at varying levels – with transition and recession.

Phalaenopsis Orchid
Roses, spray roses
Gerbera, Lysimachia
Setaria grass, Hypericum
Sedum 'Matrona', Zantedeschia
Allium, Chrysanthemum
Steel grass, Various foliages
OASIS® Foam Frames frame, Straw
Decorative reel wire, German pins

OASIS® floral adhesive

Soak frame. Begin by making the straw and Limonium forms, which are tightly bound lengths of materials (varying thicknesses) bound with fine reel wire. Also make some taped and bound wires. Secure the main pieces in place with German pins. Add groupes of materials within, above and below the structural forms. Finish with callas, steel grass and the remaining decorative forms to carry the lines through and carefully placed Phalaenopsis Orchid blooms glued in place.

Longiflorum Lilies
Rose 'Akito'
Physalis alkekengi
Various foliages
Double spray tray
OASIS® Ideal bricks
Bleached willow
Stub wire

Define the outline shape with foliage. Add willow sticks for visual interest and strength, then add the flowers in the usual manner, ensuring to recess some whilst working wiithin the framework of willow sticks.

Phalaenopsis Orchid
Hypericum
Anthurium crystallinum
Aspidistra
Steel grass
Typha latifolia
Panicum fountain
Various foliages
OASIS® Masterboard base

Soak base as usual. Begin by creating the main outline of the design with foliage – having layers and lines going softly through. Add orchids, removing individual blooms from stems which may look too heavy. Finish by adding some steel grass to keep a clean, structural and unfussy look to the completed design.

Zantedeschia aethiopica
Gypsophila
Anthurium andreanum
Covered stub wires
Fine decorative reel wire

Arrange and tie the desired amount of Arums. Taking preformed lengths of gypsophila that have been bound onto long wires, form into shape and secure. Leave plain or add rolled anthurium leaves as a design feature. Tie and cover binding point with decorative wire.

Zantedeschia aethiopica
Gypsophila paniculata
Anthurium andreanum
Covered stub wires
Fine decorative reel wire

Arrange and tie the desired amount of Arums. Taking short lengths of gypsophila that have been bound onto long wires with decorative reel wire, form into shape as desired and secure. Leave the design plain or add rolled anthurium leaves to add a different form and texture whilst still retaining the design's simplicity. Tie off and cover binding point with decorative wire.

Zantedeschia aethiopica
Molucella
Anthurium andreanum
Aspidistra
Various vines & foliages
OASIS® Masterboard base
Fine reel wire

Soak base. Start with building up an outline shape with foliage. Add Arums at varying levels. Don't forget that their stems are rather thick, so ensure that you have plenty of foam to work with and that they are positioned into the foam securely. Wire if necessary. Complete the spray by adding the rest of your foliages; some deeply recessed, others more predominant. Use rolled anthurium leaves for visual interest and to echo the flower's form and flowing grasses to soften the overall look.

Zantedeschia
Rose 'Akito'
Panicum 'Fountain'
Wild oats
Lily grass
Polybast

Prepare all materials, making sure all stems are clean and rose stems are free from foliage and thorns. Arrange Callas, roses and grasses in a hand tied fashion, keeping the stems straight. Tie the main binding point high under the flower heads and another lower down as a feature. Finish tying point by binding with lily grass.

75   Anthurium
Rose
Chrysanthemum 'Shamrock'
Chrysanthemum santini 'Yoko Ono'
Tanacetum parthenium
Hypericum
Physalis alkekengi
Amaranthus caudatus
Poppy heads

Fagus sylvatica 'Atropunicea'
Foam Frames® heart frame
Fine reel wire

Soak the frame and chamfer the edges. Mask the base with beech leaves – some face up, others face down – giving colour variation. Secure these in place with fine reel wire, taken right over and under the frame. Next add the flower materials in a textured way – making sure that materials work well together, recessing some materials.

77   Rose Sphinx, Champagne
Physalis alkekengi
Craspedia
Dianthus
Anthurium
Various foliages & bark
Foam Frames® Posy Pad
Stub wire

After preparing the frame and chamfering the edges to the desired shape, start building up your design with the central area of flowers – having grouped placements of colours, flowers and textures. Next add Aspidistra leaves to the outer edge giving a plainer area. Finish by adding softer grasses.

77   Rose
Anthurium
Asclepias
Craspedia
Chrysanthemum Santini
Physalis alkekengi
Various foilages/willow
Foam Frames® ring
Aluminium wire (copper coloured)

Start by chamfering the prepared ring. Arrange flowers & foliages in grouped placements and accentuate the form with rings of willow, decorative aluminium wire and Steel grass.

78   Helianthus
Rose 'Cherry Brandy'
Eremurus
Leucadendron
Setaria grass
Hypericum
Bleached willow
Paper covered wire
Polybast

Ribbon

First construct your framework of willow sticks, fixing with paper covered wire. Add flower materials in clean lines. Tie with polybast and finish with knotted ribbon for simplicity.

78   Helianthus
Rose 'Cherry Brandy'
Eremurus
Panicum 'Fountain'
Leucadendron
Various foliages
Eucalyptus bark
Spray tray
OASIS® Ideal brick

Prepare and soak base as usual. Build up the outline of the design with strong foliages and bark at varying levels. Add flower placements within levels, keeping a textured and more structured design.

79   Helianthus
Rose 'Cherry Brandy'
Craspedia
Leucadendron
Various foliages to include Passiflora vine & Phormium tenax.
Eucalyptus bark & willow
OASIS® posy pad base
Stub wire

Aluminum wire

Soak base and chamfer edges. Set the sunflowers at varying heights into the foam, ensuring that they are secure. Wire if in any doubt. Add Phormium leaves to outer edge, giving movement. Add other flowers and foliage in grouped placements – some recessed. Finish by adding vine, willow, wire and bark for visual interest.

80   Rose
Helianthus
Aster
Foilages
Flat moss
Wooden crate
OASIS® Ideal bricks

Secure the foam into the container, ensuring the container is lined and waterproof. Arrange flowers in a textured and grouped manner, using varying levels for visual interest. Think about what materials are being put together, so that you have plainer material next to fussy ones, making it more visually pleasing. Add flat moss if required.

.Helianthus, Roses
Sandersonia
Hydrangea, Amaranthus
Allium sphaerocephalon
Eryngium, Gypsophila
Sedum mat one
Panicum & Setaria grass
Anthurium leaves
Xanthorrhoea australis, Eucalyptus bark

Reel wire and biodegradable copper mesh

To start cut the mesh to the desired shape and size. For this piece we have chosen to decorate the central panel, so have fixed the mesh (in a slight arched form) to the willow basket with reel wire. Next prepare your flowers and foliages, including rolling the anthurium leaves. Fix the main pieces of Eucalyptus bark into place then add the rest of your flowers, foliages and grasses, weaving through the mesh and fixing in place if and when required with reel wire. Add steel grass for interest

Rose 'Passion'
Sandersonia
Physalis alkekengi
Asclepias
Panicum & Setaria grass
Various foliages
Basket
Oasis® Ideal brick
Pot Tape

Ribbon

Secure prepared foam into basket. Add foliage and flower material in usual manner. Add flowing grasses, steel grass and soft sheer flowing ribbon to visually lighter the design.

Rose 'Sphinx'
Gerbera mini
Craspedia
Physalis alkekengi
Miltonia Orchid
Viburnum opulus 'Compactum' berries
Sedum 'Matrona'
Chrysanthemum
Astilbie

Bupleurum & various foliages
Panicum 'fountain'
Foam Frames® Open Heart frame

Prepare frame as usual, chamfer edges. Start with the larger headed materials and place into the foam in groups. Carry on adding groups of smaller materials with varying textures. Complete the design by adding a few Miltonia flower heads.

Roses - David Austin® & Sphinx
Helianthus, Craspedia
Sandersonia, Limonium sinensis
Dianthus, Chrysanthemum
Miltonia Orchid
Viburnum opulus 'Compactum' berries
Sedum 'Matrona,' Setaria grass
Phomium tenax
Clematis & Passiflora vine

Straw, Reel wire, German pins, Foam Frames® ring

Begin by making the tightly bound straw forms in a variety of sizes and lengths and fix the main ones into place with German pins – the rest will be added at a later stage. Next put the Phormium leaves and some vines into the foam, giving interest and movement. Now add the flowers in clean, clear lines – keeping to the areas defined by the leaves and straw forms. Ensure that you have materials at different levels – some recessed others more prominent.

Anthurium
Gloriosa
Sandersonia
Leucadendron
Rose 'Black Baccara'
Carnation
Setaria grass
Xanthorrhoea australis
Various foliage including Phormiun tenax

Aspidistra & Ruscus
Double spray tray
Oasis® Ideal bricks
Pot tape
Cold glue

Secure foam to base tray. Start design by adding larger structural leaves to emphasise shape. Add flower materials at varying levels, in lines through the spray. Accentuate the shape by adding steel grass.

Gerbera
Dianthus
Miltonia Orchid
Viburnum opulus 'Compactum' berries
Hypericum
Fagus sylvatica 'Atropunicea'
Xanthorrhoea australis
Foam Frames® wreath frame
Fine decorative reel wire

Prepare frame in the usual way then chamfer the edges to give a good profile. Base the pillow with beech leaves – alternative sides for colour interest. Secure in place with fine reel wire. Add design feature to the pillow with textured placements of materials. Finish with threaded berries and steel grass chains, for soften the overall effect.

Rose 'Passion'
Clematis vine
Muehlenbeckia
Hedera
Biodegradable Cross frame
Reel wire

Prepare the frame and chamfer edges. Start with placing the main "cross" of roses into the foam. Next add a selection of trailing foliages to the frame, together with some shorter foliages and rose calyxes. Finish by adding Clematis vine and garlands of rolled rose petals around the frame.

89 Rose 'Passion'
Xanthorrhoea australis
Basket
Oasis® Ideal bricks
Polybast
Oasis® Floral adhesive

Secure soaked foam into lined basket. Insert roses into the foam keeping a good amount of foliage on the stems to mask foam. Add steel grass for interest and movement and finish by gluing a few rose petals to the steel grass.

90 Anthurium, Gerbera mini
Amaranthus,
Eryngium
Hypericum,
Zantedeschia
Viburnum opulus 'Compactum' berries
Various foliages including Fagus sylvatica & Aspidistra.
Hay

Basket
OASIS® Ideal bricks
Paper covered wire
Reel wire

Fix soaked foam into bsket, (ensuring that it is well lined) and insert foliage giving an outline to the design. Add flower material and finish with a few lengths of hay forms which have been tightly bound with decorative reel wire, which adds interest and brings colours through.

91 Lily 'Sorbonne'
Anthurium
Gerbera mini
Amaranthus
Hypericum
Viburnum opulus 'Compactum' berries
Anthurium crystallinum & andreanum,
Various foliages to include Aspidestra,
Ruscus

OASIS® Masterboard
Decorative reel wire

Prepare the frame, roll Anthurium andreanum leaves and fix with decorative reel wire and put to one side. Take the main foliages and insert into foam defining the outline shape of the spray. Next add the flower material and fill with shorter foliages including the rolled leaves and flat Anthurium crystallinum leaves for visual interest and a varying texture within the design.

92 David Austin® Rose 'Miranda'
Rose 'Cool Water'
Spray Rose 'Sereno' & 'Diadeem'
Muehlenbeckia base
OASIS®
Skeleton band
Reel wire
Sisal

Shape the vine into desired shape and add soaked foam section to the centre. Secure into place. Add mixed shapes, forms, size and colour onto the design. Finish with skeleton band and sisal fibres to soften and accentuate the heart shape.

93 David Austin® Roses (various varieties)
Gypsophila
Lysimachia
Allium sphaerocephalon
Ammi majus
Tanacetum parthenium
Amaranthus
Setaria and Panicum 'Fountain' grass
OASIS® designer board

Sisal

First mark out the chosen form onto the designer sheet and cut out. Soak the frame and chamfer the edges, giving a good profile. Mark the outer section and mask with gyp, ensuring a good, dense coverage. Next add the main flower placements at varying levels, using a mix of varying flower forms – round, spray, arching, creating more visual interest.

94 Dianthus barbatus
Peperomia
Phormium tenax
Euonymus
Setaria grass
Xanthorrhoea australis
Foam Frames® Posy pad frame

After preparing the frame, chamfer the edges, then add the Phormium leaf to the outer edge and fix. Next insert the Sweet Williams into the posy pad, keeping a flat profile. Finally decorate the design with leaves and grasses.

94 Godetia
Dianthus barbatus
Setaria grass
Xanthorrhoea australis
Wild Oats
Phormium tenax
Muehlenbeckia
Alchemilla mollis
Passiflora vine &various grasses

Foam Frames® wreath frame

Prepare the frame and chamfer the edges. Roughly mask the frame with foliage and mixed grasses, then add the Phormium leaves as a solid clean line within the design. Next add the main flower placements of Godetia & Sweet William, with plenty of recession and depth. Finish by softening the overall look with the wild Oats, passion flower vine and steel grass, in a circular movement accentuating the wreath form and symbolism.

95

Fagus sylvatica 'Atropunicea'
Rose
Gloriosa
Amaranthus
Pepper berries
Phormium tenax
Foam Frames® Heart frame
Decorative reel wire

After soaking and chamfering the frame to the desired profile, cover the base with Beech leaves, securing in place with reel wire. For interest on one side, add some cut pieces of Phormium leaf. On the other opposite side, a bold, textured and interesting spray of Roses, Gloriosa, Amaranthus and Pepper berries.

97

Viburnum opulus 'Compactum' berries
Xanthorrhoea australis
Hypericum berries
Cornus
Birch bark (hessian backed on a roll)
Foam Frames® cross frame
Black pins

After soaking the frame, attach the Birch bark to the outer edge with black pins, making sure that you insert some pins into the harder base for security. Next add the berries, keeping a compact and flat profile and inside the birch edge. Add a few strands of Steel grass to the top to emphasise the cross form and finish with a garland of berries, Cornus and Steel grass.

97

Viburnum opulus 'Compactum' berries
Gloriosa
Gerbera mini
Dianthus
Amaranthus
Birch bark (hessian backed on a roll)
Foam Frames® cross frame
Black pins

Ribbon

After soaking the frame, attach the Birch bark to the outer edge with black pins. Add a berry to the pin for decoration and make sure that you insert some pins into the harder base for security. Next add the berries and flowers, with variation in the levels to create visual interest. Ensure that the flower placements are all inside the birch edging. Add Amaranthus trails and fine satin ribbon lengths to soften.

98

Various winter foliages including Conifer, Quercus
Poppy heads
Physalis alkekengi
Birch & Willow
Wild Oats
Cones, nuts and bark
Skeleton leaves
Cinnamon

Straw ring
Decorated stub wires (taped & bound with reel wire)
German pins and stub wires

Lay the main flatter materials onto the ring and secure in place with German pins. Next add cones, cinnamon, bark curls and long willow & birch twigs for bulk, texture and movement in the design. Add more foliages if required. Then emphasize the form with decorative wires. Finish the design with a simple ribbon of birch bark.

99

Anthurium
Chrysanthemum
Physalis alkekengi
Antirrhinum
Hypericum
Amaranthus
Panicum 'fountain'
Convolvulus arvensis
Birch (twigs & roll)

Biodegradable mesh
Reel wire

Secure the mesh to the coffin with reel wire, giving a base to work onto. Strip the leaves from the bindweed, then lay on the mesh and fix in place. Add your other flower and foliage materials and fix. To finish, add more bindweed to soften and length of birch ribbon.

100

Winter foliages – Taxus baccata, Conifer, Ilex
Various cones
Cinnamon
Lunaria pennies
Bark
Bear grass (Gold)
Foam Frames® ring
Angel Hair

Stub wires
OASIS® Floral adhesive

Soak and chamfer the frame. Insert foliage in usual way. Add cones, cinnamon and bark and soften with a flourish of gold bear grass and angel hair. Honesty pennies are glued to finish.

101

Ilex
Rose 'Passion'
Leucadendron
Conifer "cones"
Xanthorrhoea australis
Foam Frames® ring
Black pins

Soak and chamfer the frame. Working an area at a time, add the base layer of holly leaves to the frame securing in place with pins. When circle is complete, add another layer, with leaves at a different angle for interest, ensuring that all of the foam is covered. Insert a single rose and a flourish of steel grass to enhance. Roll single petals and secure in place with a pin. Add Leucadendron leaves – some whole leaves, others folded and a mix of conifer and Hypericum berries.

BOTANICAL/COMMON NAMES

Agapanthus – African lily
Alstroemeria – Peruvian lily
Amaranthus caudatus – Cat's tail
Anthurium – Flamingo flower/painter's palette
Antirrhinum – Snapdragon
Aspidistra elatior – Cast iron plant
Centaurea cyanus– Cornflower
Chamelaucium uncinatum – Waxflower
Convallaria majalis - Lily of the Valley
Dendranthema – Chrysanthemum
Dianthus - Carnation
Dianthus barbatus - Sweet William
Eremurus stenophyllus – Foxtail lily
Eryngium – Sea holly
Eustoma Russell – Lisianthus
Gerbera – Transvaal daisy
Gloriosa rothschildiana – Glory lily
Gypsophila paniculata – Baby's breath
Helianthus – Sunflower
Hypericum – St John's wort
Ilex – Holly
Lathyrus odoratus – Sweet pea
Liatris spicata – Button snakeroot
Limonium overig – sea lavender
Lysimachia clethroides – Loosestrife
Myosotis – forget me not
Physostegia virginiana – Obedient flower
Rosa - Rose
Sandersonia aurantiaca – Chinese lantern lily
Strelitzia reginae – Bird of paradise
Tanacetum parthenium – Matricaria
Triteleia - Brodiaea
Viburnum opulus 'Roseum' – Snowball, Guelder rose
Xerophyllum tenax – bear grass
Xanthorrhoea – steel grass
Zantedeschia aethiopica – Calla

ROSE

Wow! What a flower this is. The types and varieties are so diverse, the colours and forms scrumptious. The message they convey is always the same – they are for someone very special. Choose the type, colour, size, form and variety carefully depending on the required effect and use. Use mixes of size, colour and form selectively. Whole flowers of varying sizes and stages of maturity

en masse are gorgeous used as a basing material. Use lots of individual petals bound in place with very fine reel wire but avoid using varieties which have very soft petals as they are liable to bruise easily. Roll petals and wire them onto reel wire to make strings of petals, twisting several strings together. Stack them lei fashion onto reel wire and incorporate into designs. Use rosehips when available. Large thorns make excellent natural fixings. Red is the classic flower of love, white for purity and spiritual love, yellow for friendship.

CARNATIONS

Cheap, cheerful and oh so versatile! So why is it that the poor old carnation has such an image problem? Carnations have been cultivated for over two thousand years, were reputedly used to make garlands in ancient Greece and are just perfect for all kinds of design work right now. And what's more, they're available in a huge range of colours, all the year round. They make a

quick and effective basing material – split the calyx and pin the whole carnation down as an alternative to just inserting it in foam – the petals merge together better. Decorate to suit – with a complementary spray, surrounded with a vine collar, or a floral ribbon. Use individual petals glued onto floral ribbons. Short lengths of cut stem, bound onto decorative reel wire in long strings are great for making trails and tails. Use discarded calyxes in the same way. Sensitive to ethylene.

CHRYSANTHEMUM

A traditional flower – firmly associated with the rather staid kind of basing so popular in the last decade or two. Look past those old-fashioned techniques and discover a new and really useful material. Check out the modern varieties, cool new colours. Use trendy small varieties as a base, but use them at different heights rather than the pristine flat bases of times gone by. Make long strings

by threading small flowers and buds onto decorative wire, twist together and use them in cascading trails. Use gorgeous large headed blooms protected with a twig frame as an alternative to a tied posy or sheaf. Great for autumnal work with their distinctive scent and colour range.

Chrysanthemums are a traditional flower of mourning and grief.

FILLER FLOWERS

Necessary to cover mechanics and add volume. Loads of choice depending on colour, season and form required. Ammi majus, Alchemilla mollis, Aster ericoides (September flower), Hypericum, Solidago, Solidaster, Waxflower, Limonium, Gypsophila, Tanacetum parthenium, lots of the "Safari mix" Leucadendron; Mimosa... the list is endless! Use recessed and in small

clusters in fairly traditional work. Several types are also well suited to being used for cloud like basing or garlanding. Use generously for best effect. Important to consider texture, form and colour for great results. Good filler foliages include Hebe, Myrtle, Rosemary, lots of the Eucalyptus and Viburnum family, Salal.

GYPSOPHILA

Love or loathe it gypsophila is one of the most useful materials around, available all year round, in white and pink. Although it has a rather staid image it is still a decorative material which has lots of possibilities. Use en masse as a basing material as an alternative to AYR, then decorate accordingly – perhaps with a spray to one side, or using a different kind of flower to punctuate the form at

regular intervals. Or perhaps drape a floral ribbon right across the tribute. Gypsophila is also great for edgings – make sure that it is used densely for best effect. Sometimes it is far quicker to wire small bundles than to insert them individually. It may also be used to make fine, tightly bound garlands which are excellent to add an accent to work. And of course to use as a regular 'filler flower' but only in the nicest possible way!! Cut between nodes, use cut flower food. It is sensitive to ethylene.

ORCHIDS

This huge family of flower material is fabulous to use and the cost is always money well spent as the blooms add a touch of luxury and opulence to a design. White Phalaenopsis are classically beautiful, whilst Cymbidium tend to be more modestly priced. If using whole stems look at them carefully – it may be possible to remove a few blooms (which may be used elsewhere as an

accent flower), which makes the stem look more balanced and less clumpy and solid, and beneficial financially. Dendrobiums are great to use on the stem or threaded onto steel grass for a different effect. Individual blooms may be fastened onto decorative wires using a dab of cold glue to add a luxurious touch to more simple design concepts. The curiously shaped Paphiopedilum is gorgeous to use as an accent flower on a simple woven wreath for example.

ARUM/ZANTEDESCHIA

A traditional flower of mourning used throughout the centuries and which are suitable for a wide range of design possibilities. Zantedeschia are gorgeous used in simple hand tied designs which may be decorated in lots of ways to add a modern twist. A few carefully placed distinctive leaves gives structure. Alternatively use in classic sprays with nicely textured materials - guelder

rose, hypericum, or roses, perhaps? Coloured Zantedeschia are ideal for using as focal flowers in a clean, unfussy way. Stems may be gently arched to enable curves to be made.

LILIES

Longiflorum lilies are excellent for use in large scale sprays. Order in advance of requirement to allow flowers to develop and mature. Remove pollen before using as it has a nasty tendency to stain petals. Use some buds as well as open flowers for transition and best effect.

MOSSES

Bun moss and flat moss are the most widely used mosses in funeral designs. Make sure it is purchased from a sustainable source, never gather in the wild as it is protected and you'll be liable to a fine. Clean moss carefully, removing all pieces of stick and debris. Bun moss often needs to have the depth removed using a sharp knife. If the colour has faded a bit, dip into boiling water for a few

VINES & TRAILS

A huge and never ending choice available and often free! Wisteria, clematis, bindweed, rubus, honeysuckle, passion flower, ivy, wild hop vine... clippings from all these and dozens of other plants provide excellent material with which to create loops, rustic bases, posy frames and cascades over and through designs. Look at the texture, colour and structure of the stem,

LEAVES

Large leaves add distinction and a design statement. Currently popular are Anthurium, Aspidistra, Fatsia, Alocasia and Cordyline, 'Miss Brown' is a favourite with its smoky brown leaf edged in gold. Use leaves in a variety of ways – Anthurium are good rolled and fastened with decorative reel wire, or used as a cone for enclosing a small posy. Fasten tidily with cold glue. Aspidistra are handy

FOLIAGE

Used as a filler to enhance the flower material small leaved types are usually best – including lots of the Hebe's, Myrtle, viburnum, box, bay and eucalyptus. Individual leaves stacked lei fashion make an interesting alternative to cascade over works. Cover bases with leaves for an individual effect. Good things to try are beech, Stachys lanata, Eleagnus, ivy. These could be fastened individually

moments. This will make the colour intensify again for a while. Use moss as areas of quiet in textured designs. Sometimes it is easier to scoop a little of the foam base off to accommodate the depth of the moss, but beware – once it's removed it's not easy to change your mind. Trailing Tillandsia is perfect for using sparingly as a base on which to nestle a choice bloom.

whether it is knobbly or smooth, shiny or rough. The easily found weed – bindweed – is absolutely great for stripping and using as a natural trail. It dries well too. Strip all the leaves off and use as you please. Other materials may include fine Muehlenbeckia which can be used in loads of ways – fresh, massed as a delicate edging. Dried, it's good as a base for hand fashioned collars, bases and accents.

to split and use for covering large areas quickly and cost effectively. Leaves such as Galax or large ivy leaves are great for posy pad designs. Autumnal leaves are superb for loads of design ideas. Use coloured leaves as normal, or scrunched up as a base on which to add materials. They are also great for winter and spring work grouped with lichened twigs and delicate bulb flowers. Smaller leaves can be snugly bound onto bases with decorative reel wire, and then finished as appropriate.

with pins or German pins or bound on with decorative reel wire. The finished effect could be regular or random depending on the type, size, colour and texture of leaves chosen. Ensure the leaves are of a suitable size so that they are in proportion to the whole piece. Use well conditioned foliage which is clean, use leaf shine if you feel it appropriate and adds to the overall design. Often I prefer a natural sheen as opposed to a high gloss.

FINE LEAVES & GRASSES

Versatile materials open up lots of design possibilities. Old favourites like bear grass, steel grass and flexigrass are great to use for accentuating the form. Use to highlight the flowers by adding a flourish, or in the case of steel grass folding over and through the design. Make decorative collars with bear grass. China grass, typha grass and Ophiopogon are excellent for weaving as an

alternative to a floral base material. Phormium is great for structural designs, also to split lengthwise for weaving – discard the central spine section. Also there are dozens of gorgeous grasses to use which add a casual country garden feel to work – favourites include Panicum 'Fountain,' Wild Oats, Wheat and Harestail's. Oh, and then there's hay and straw – which is wonderful for making a bed for other materials, or crescents tied tightly with decorative reel wire and incorporated into designs.

BERRIES & FRUITS

Berries and fruits add a whole new dimension and open up hundreds of design possibilities. They include day to day things like Hypericum as well as gorgeous treasures such as Viburnum berries, ivy berries, Symphoricarpos, rose hips. Use them as a different texture throughout casual pieces alternatively use them as the main material, where their colour and form is truly appreci-

ated. Berries and small fruits work particularly well with bark, veneer and scrunched up autumn leaves. Throughout the year there are hundreds of seed heads and fruits to choose from - the common to imported specialities. How about poppy seed heads, Nigella, pepper berries, Myrtle, blackberries, elderberries and crab apples for starters?

CONES & DRIED

Great for winter and Christmas time designs, varying from the small Larch cones on long arching branches to the large specimen cones from the Cedar and pines. Use them as an accent, or a base. Sometimes good to use upside down for a completely different effect. Other drieds that are useful are cinnamon sticks – available in a wide variety of lengths, Lunaria (honesty pennies),

skeletonized leaves (of varying sizes and colours – especially bleached) and star anise. Freshly dried autumn leaves are superb for using as bases in autumn work, choose a variety of sizes, colours and shapes. Store in a cool dry place until required.

STICKS & TWIGS

Use various types of sticks as accents or to make protective frames for simple hand tieds. Alternatively use them to make simple crosses to be decorated with strings of small flowers. Gnarled, rugged pieces of lichen covered twig create interest especially when used in winter, spring and autumnal works. Fruitwood twigs are particularly good to use. Cornus is perfect to use

throughout the winter, as its colourful stems add a pleasant contrast to the flower material. Deck reed is excellent for using in cut lengths and wired onto decorative reel wire, to make cascading trails. Birch bark used in sections is superb for rustic works, as is fine birch bark ribbon used as an edging or finishing flourish. Eucalyptus bark curls adds texture. Bamboo is superb for making natural crosses - sepecially nigra. Bind stems together and finish with a flower of simple form!

TEXTURAL MATERIALS

Developing a keen sense of what textures go together well is a skill which should be continually developed. Make a habit of putting groups of materials together (not necessarily floral) and seeing what effects come about – retro, traditional, classical, modern, clashing, contrasting. Some ideas will work, some won't. Textured materials can be found in all the categories listed

TROPICALS

Under this heading are lots of useful materials which are both exciting to use and contemporary in nature. Anthuriums have fascinating and gorgeously textured spathes to use as accents, where a simple yet dramatic design is required. Their intense colour range is perfect for young people, whilst the brown and green are highly suited to masculine tributes that are clean and structured. They

COUNTRY GARDEN

Flowers reminiscent of country gardens evoke strong emotions and are perfect for using in casual abundance. Old fashioned flowers such as Godetia, Sweet William, garden pinks, Scabious and marguerites are firm favourites and best used simply without too much fuss. Others include Larkspur, Delphinium, peony, old fashioned blowsy roses, forget me nots, Tanacetum

BINDING & BEDDING

Sisal, coconut fibre, linen watten, raffia, offcuts of natural leather and various strings are all useful for adding texture into design and bedding down choice flowers in minimalist pieces. A band of sisal is great for covering the tying point on hand tieds and as a wispy material used sparingly through designs. Do not make the mistake of using colours are not always waterproof - beware! Raffia

   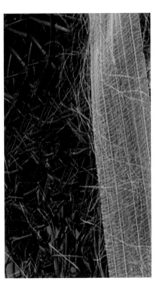

here and more besides. Favourites include Eryngium – various species – Sedum, Echeveria (loads of varieties), Trachelium, Amaranthus, Viburnum opulus 'Roseum,' Celosia, mosses, Craspedia, gnarled twigs... different things in different seasons, and for different effects.

make an effective token tribute when teamed up with a few fine leaves. Protea are such strong looking flowers yet so delicate and tactile to the touch. Prone to bruising, so great care should be taken in their conditioning and handling. Gorgeous to use as a small tribute decorated in some way. They are also great to dissect so that the furry stamens can be used as a design feature. Other favourites include Berzelia, Brunia albiflora and the curious Leucospermum.

parthenium and dill. Lots of volume is preferable to over complicated designs for the majority of these types of material. Loose, informal styling is preferable to highly detailed.

is just right for a country garden styling and for casual bunches. Dried Muehlenbeckia is excellent for making natural bases, tease it out and secure the shape with reel wire. Use fresh Muehlenbeckia to mask frames and underneath accent flowers. Suedette cord is a gorgeous new material for tying that's bang up to date. Strings, ropes of various thicknesses and cords are great as design features, and which can lead the eye into and round a design.

SPRING

Tributes in the springtime have an amazing array of materials available from Muscari, through to hyacinth, tulips, daffodils, anemones and ranunculus. It may be appropriate to incorporate scrunched up leaves, bursting twigs and bulbs as well as flowers and foliage to signify nature's cycle of death and renewal. Catkins, pussy willow and colourful stems of Cornus are gorgeous textures and

forms to include. It may be that potted primroses, violets or bellis could be planted into rustic, woodlandy type designs. Other things which are current favourites of ours throughout this season include the gorgeous Fritillaria meleagris, Cheerfulness, Helleborus argutifolius and H. orientalis. An added bonus is that so many of these gems are scrumptiously fragrant.

SUMMER

Summer means abundance and during the long hot days meadow flowers and country garden flowers seem highly appropriate to use. Cornflowers, marguerites (my all time favourite), cosmos, dahlia, sweet William, godetia, peony, roses (all kinds in abundance – dog roses, moss roses, old fashioned roses, commercial roses – standard and spray), phlox and hydrangea. All are

absolutely gorgeous to use and offer endless design possibilities. None however warrant the constraints of being subjected to stiff, contrived design. Loose and casual designs are preferable every time.

Poppies in their delicate clear colours are fragile and ethereal and simply stunning teamed up with some poppy seed heads and wispy grasses.

AUTUMN

Seasonal chrysanthemums, with their distinctive scent, fruits, berries and gorgeously coloured leaves evoke feelings of autumn. Physalis alkekengi are superb for a different textural effect, whether green or the more usual orange. Berries in their glorious colours and textures provide countless ideas for bases as well as being ideal for threading onto long lengths of deco-

rative reel wire, and over designs. Rich golds, russets and bronzes are the perfect colour palette to use. Sunflowers with their cheerful happy faces are excellent as a token or included in larger works and ideal for younger people. Blackberry stems offer brilliant colour combinations as their fruits turn from soft green, through to red and black.

WINTER

Lots of evergreens teamed up with a few choice flowers make long lasting and emotive tributes. Try using greenery with a few stems of Helleborus niger or a selection of cones and berries for a classic tribute. Holly, box, Myrtle, Larch cone stems, Cedrus, pine, Thuja and Abies are easily available and excellent to use. Further ideas may be to base with one kind of greenery then add a deco-

rated ribbon of berries and seedheads across the middle. Also good to use pieces of bark, stems such as Cornus and Willow.

THANKS A BUNCH!

We have received some generous sponsorship for our new sympathy book, we hope they like our creations. We are hugely grateful for their generosity.

David Austin® Roses supplied us with an abundance of their gorgeous English garden roses, some of them so new they still had not been named! Using them to produce an emotive collection of tributes has been an absolute pleasure, and their shape, form and fragrance is unforgettable. We have ideas for many many more designs! What wonderful flowers for truly emotive tributes. Thank you so, so much.

David Austin® Roses, Bowling Green Lane, Albrighton, Wolverhampton, WV7 3HB, ENGLAND
Tel: 0044 (0)1902 376 301
Web: www.davidaustinroses.com e-mail: cutflowers@davidaustinroses.com

Smithers Oasis® generously supplied us with a fabulous range of their hugely popular frames and sundries. The use of foam frames makes the florist's job so quick and easy as well as ensuring that flower material remains fresh and in prime condition for the occasion required. We have so many ideas for so many more pieces.... ! Thank you so much for your tremendous support in this project. It is very much appreciated.

Smithers-Oasis U.K. Ltd. Crowther Road, Crowther Industrial Estate, Washington, Tyne & Wear, NE 38 0AQ, ENGLAND.
Tel: 0044 (0) 1914 175 595
web: www.smithersoasis.com e-mail: UKinfo@smithersoasis.com

ABOUT US

Our aim is simply to promote fine floristry! This may be directly to a client or through influencing others; sharing knowledge, skills, design ideas, concerns and enthusiasm - enabling others to increase their own appreciation of flowers and nature.

2006 – launched thrive floristry, a specialist company dedicated to promoting our style of floristry, our flower school and bespoke floral design. Webshop selling a wide range of floristic products and books from around the world, as well as our own.
Check it out at www.thrivefloristry.com

BOOKS & PUBLICATIONS
2005 – Claire featured in the International Annual of Floral Art 05/06 as one of the selected UK designers
2003 – Straight from the Heart – bridal floristry for the 21st century
2002 - Claire featured in Best of British – a celebration of inspirational
      floristry
      Straight from the Heart – bridal floristry for the 21st century
      Straight from the Heart – sympathy floristry for the 21st
      century
1995 featured in A Christmas Feast – Anton Edelmann

Work featured in numerous magazines and publications, including: Fusion Flowers Weddings, Fusion Flowers, Flora International, Wedding Flowers magazine and lots more

ACCOLADES
Three times RHS Chelsea Gold medallists. One time Best in Show.
One time RHS Chelsea Silver Medallist

PROFESSIONAL QUALIFICATIONS
Liz - National Diploma of the Society of Floristry
Claire - Intermediate Certificate of the Society of Floristry

ACKNOWLEDGEMENTS

Every journey starts but with a single step... classic advice! Our journey with this book has been an eventful one; what with the photography sessions being during the exhausting temperatures in one of our hottest summer's on record (albeit short lived!). Decisions, decisions, decisions – on format, layout, what to include, what not to include. Seeing the pages come together to create a book of which to be proud and which we sincerely hope will be of positive benefit to the industry – students and florist's alike. Our work concentrate on sensual and evocative designs to reflect the prevailing mood in the world, current trends and the growing appreciation of nature and all it has to offer.

Our grateful and sincere thanks go to David Austin® Roses, who generously provided their classic English roses, to Smithers Oasis® who generously sponsored the foam frames and other sundries and to Nick Armstrong for the loan of coffins. It is very much appreciated. Thank you once again to Peter Griffin at GGS Creative Graphics and Richard Parrington at Reflex Litho for their expertise. We like to support local companies and thank them for supporting us in our vision and adventure, and providing service with a smile.

Last, but certainly not least, we must thank everyone at home. Ben for the smart and unfussy layout – ALWAYS the hours are unconventional (nothing like the normal 9 – 5 around here), but who cares?! We are extremely proud to think that this is Ben's book no. 4! To Jane and Rachel for proof reading, and to the Mums who have been so patient and supportive of us throughout the realization of all our dreams, whether successful, harebrained or otherwise!

It has been a long journey, and like the journey of life, has had its ups and downs, sunshine and showers. We hope you too take pleasure in a lifelong journey of appreciating flowers, and enjoy their diversity and the unlimited possibilities that they present every day.

BIBLIOGRAPHY

Decorative Cut Flowers – Coen Gelein & Nees Joore – 1988

Flower Council of Holland

Plantscope

INDEX

SYMPATHY COLLECTION